THE WEALTH LIFESTYLE:

Discover a New Retirement, Live and Work with the Freedom You Desire

BY STEVEN MICHAEL ENGLAND

THE WEALTH LIFESTYLE:
Discover a New Retirement, Live and Work with the Freedom You Desire

ISBN: 978-1-7325893-8-4

Printed in the United States of America
Year of First Printing: 2020

Dedication

To my beautiful wife, Cindi, who has stood by my side through it all, and my incredible children, Daren, Matthew, Leah, Paige, and Brooke.

Acknowledgements

I'd like to say "thank you" to my wonderful clients that have become my extended family and who I respect so very much. Thank you, Hal Price, my faithful friend, business partner, and brother in Christ for over twenty years. Thank you to Marvin Bowers, my friend and associate; to Bill and Sandy Fischer, my friends that got me into Motorcycling in West Virginia for the best of memories; to my brother Alan, a retired firefighter who is one of the hardest working men I know; to Brett Kitchen who told me I could write a book; to Shannon who listened and helped me tell my story; to Lee who coordinated it all; and thank you to every person that I met with, listened to, and talked to over thirty years that gave me the insights and stories of my life's work.

About the Author

I have thirty-eight years of financial services experience, and have worked with hundreds of families, creating Wealth Lifestyle strategies for their retirement. Over the course of my career, I have been on three boards of large financial services companies, and I am among the top 1 percent sales advisors in my field. Upwards of 95 percent of all my clients do additional business with me or refer me to someone they know. I attribute my success to my unique hands-on approach; I have dedicated my life to the people I serve, and my clients have direct access to me at all times.

Reviews and Testimonials

"Occasionally, God presents you with the honor of having someone in your corner that means much greater impact on our lives than originally envisioned. Steven is that person. Not only does he have extensive financial investment knowledge but is willing to share that knowledge by offering proven and reliable products and services that cater to your unique financial goals. This book demonstrates the sincerity of Steven's heart toward demonstrating his love for God and sharing it throughout all areas of his life, both professionally and personally."

-Dennis and Kathleen Lindsay

"I have known and worked with Steve for about fifteen years. He is a Christian and family man that cares for his clients. I have never known him to look at or care about what he would make in offering a product to a client. Service is primary and keeping up to date with changes in the industry is of the utmost importance. I have said at some group meetings we have held, if Steve says something you can take it to the bank. His only statement is, 'If the market falls, you may not make anything, but you will never lose a dime.' I consider him not only an associate, but a good friend as well."

-Marvin and Shirley Bowers

"I wish we could have read this book years ago, the book is full of sound advice, and principals that work to protect your life's savings while providing you a stress-free retirement."

-Willie and Sandy Fisher

"Mr. England's knack for storytelling shines through in his latest book, *The Wealth Lifestyle*, and more importantly, his well-earned financial acumen results in a valuable paradigm shift for investor consideration. This is especially true for those nearing retirement in this new financial age. It is a valuable contribution to the financial marketplace of ideas."

-Scott Parker

Table of Contents

ACKNOWLEDGEMENTS....4

ABOUT THE AUTHOR....5

REVIEWS AND TESTIMONIALS....6

FOREWORD....11

CHAPTER 1

THERE'S MORE TO LIFE THAN MONEY....17

CHAPTER 2

DEVELOPING THE WEALTH LIFESTYLE....29

CHAPTER 3

RETIREMENT HAS CHANGED....39

CHAPTER 4

COVERING YOUR BASES....53

CHAPTER 5

TAX FREE RETIREMENT....63

CHAPTER 6

THE WEALTH LIFESTYLE METHOD.....73

CHAPTER 7

WHAT'S STOPPING YOU?.....81

CHAPTER 8

PROTECTING YOUR ASSETS.....89

CHAPTER 9

LEAVING A TAX ADVANTAGED LEGACY.....103

CHAPTER 10

NOW IS THE TIME TO DREAM.....113

CHAPTER 11

LET'S GET STARTED.....121

FOREWORD

A few years after graduating from university in 1986, I began my investment and trading journey. The following year I experienced my first 34 percent swing in the market. Even with this significant correction, I enjoyed the excitement of being engaged in the markets. Since then, I, like many of you, have lived through the ups and downs of the tech bubble bursting, the 2008 meltdown, and the 2010 flash crash. Even with the back and forth swings of the market, I have continued to enjoy investing my own money.

In February 2020, as the Dow dropped 9,000 points in four weeks, I started thinking this wasn't quite as fun and exciting as it was in my 30s and 40s. Around this time, a banner popped up on my computer, it was an internet ad talking about investing in annuities as a safer alternative. Frankly, I've never been that interested in insurance or annuity products, but I requested more information anyway. A month later, I met Steve England for the first time.

Our first phone call was a pleasant surprise. I thought for sure he was going to pitch his products to me. Instead,

Steve wanted to hear all about me and my family, our dreams, and desires. Steve listened—really listened. Very quickly, I came to find out that we shared many values, but most importantly, we had the common fundamental belief that there was more to life than money. Over the next few months, Steve and I built a new friendship.

Eventually, the subject of annuities and insurance products did come up, but we also talked about many other things. It was during these conversations when Steve shared with me that he was working on a book project. At the time, he was unaware I had served as managing director of the Halftime Institute and had worked directly with Bob Buford. (Bob is the author of *Halftime,* as well as numerous other books that deal with making a significant impact in the second half of your life.) So, when Steve asked if I'd be interested in reading the pre-release of his book and writing a foreword, I told him I would love to.

Here's what I found in this book and why I think you will enjoy reading it as well. Unlike other finance books, Steve's emphasis is not only on making money for yourself and your family but also making an impact in the world around you. It struck me. I found myself excited about the book's potential influence on individuals as they thought about the last quarter of their life. Steve's personal story and his receptive approach to helping people with their finances was refreshing. His explanations of various "safe money" strategies, including the use of insurance and annuities, were engaging. For someone who has never had any interest in either, getting me engaged in this part of the book is quite a feat! Most of all, I love how Steve laid out examples of individuals who are impacting the world with their finances and the tangible step-by-step methods of how they got there.

Ten years ago, I had my own "halftime revelation" and, as a result, co-founded Edify. Our mission is to improve and expand sustainable Christ-centered education globally. Currently, we work in eleven countries in Africa, Latin America, and India. At Edify, we have the privilege of coming alongside everyday men and women who have started very low-fee independent schools in their communities. It is an honor and privilege to hear their stories of sacrifice, and how they use the little earthly resources they have to make a massive impact on the children in their communities and beyond. I see the joy in their eyes as they share how they've been called to make a difference. They truly are living out their dreams and callings!

It is because of this work that I believe Steve is committed to helping others live out their dreams and their callings, too. I am confident that you'll enjoy reading this book as much as I have. But proceed with caution, it has the potential to dramatically change the way you approach the rest of your life.

Tiger Dawson

CEO and Co-founder of Edify

CHAPTER 1

THERE'S MORE TO LIFE THAN MONEY

When I saw the professional job the garage had done, I was thrilled.

My father-in-law looked at me, then looked at the car, and back at me again; he had a big grin on his face. "Let's take her for a drive!"

It was the end of winter, in March of 1995. I had just gotten some work done on my car and I was standing in the driveway with my father-in-law watching it be delivered. My father-in-law loved cars and owned a GNX Grand National himself. He lived a couple hours away, but he drove down in the morning because he wanted to be there when they unloaded it.

When the car arrived, we took a moment to inspect it. The dealership was known for its custom work, and they definitely didn't disappoint. I had just bought the car a few months ago, a 1995 Dodge Viper, black on black. I didn't have anything major done, just some silver striping custom painted on the hood and wrapped around the back. Also, they increased the performance of the car with custom exhaust and performance upgrades.

> "It all happened in less than two seconds — we actually sailed 30 feet through the air, going about 80 miles an hour, Dukes of Hazzard style."

We climbed into the car and took off. Both my father-in-law and I are sports car enthusiasts, but I definitely didn't want to hurt myself or my car, so I was taking it pretty easy. We'd been out for about thirty-five minutes cruising the backroads near my house. On our way back, I turned onto a road that wound around a large lake. There was a long sweeping corner coming up, and as I got onto it, I shifted from second to third. When I did, the car suddenly came around on me. It just snapped and lifted up off the ground as it rounded the corner too quickly. The car had Positraction with no electronic assists, so it's very easy to wreck, and I'd just had work done on it, so she had 100 plus more horsepower than I was used to. By the time I corrected the car, we were in a ditch headed toward a large culvert.

It all happened in less than two seconds—we actually sailed thirty feet through the air, going about eighty miles an hour, Dukes of Hazzard style. My father-in-law had his seat belt on, but I didn't, so I went right through the cloth top and hit the top bar that was just above the windshield, clear over the rear view mirror, scraping my head on the top of the car. I climbed out of the wreck. The metal bar had peeled half of my scalp back— I'd actually scalped myself— and I was bleeding profusely. My father-in-law was on the ground, rolling around in pain. The seat belt had injured his ribs badly, and he couldn't breathe. The pain was intense, but it didn't knock me out. I sat down in front of my totaled, steaming, smashed up car and waited for the ambulance to arrive.

Luckily, the ambulance was only four minutes from where we were when they got the call. They got there fast. Later, they told me if they had been any further away, I would have bled out. On that ambulance ride to the hospital, I had the strangest experience. I was fully awake, but close to death. At that moment, I felt myself slipping away. Some people say they see their loved ones, or even angels— but laying there on the gurney, I saw the brightest, warmest, most beautiful light I've ever seen. I just wanted to go there so badly, it was drawing me in. But I couldn't.

I couldn't go because I knew my priorities weren't straight. I didn't have the Lord in my life. ALSO, I was very close to my wife and I knew she would be devastated if I left her behind.

I didn't have time to ponder it too deeply, I just knew what I experienced. When they got me into the hospital, they sewed me up. Fortunately, I didn't break any bones, but I had a crazy head laceration, and a concussion. That was it. When I got back home, the ambulance and rescue people who saved me came to my house to make sure I was okay. None of them thought I was going to make it. They were really concerned.

To this day I can still vividly remember hitting that culvert, hard. It totaled the car, and the force of it pushed the V-10 engine and transmission back fourteen inches. I was truly lucky to be alive. But this feeling wouldn't last long.

Three weeks later, I had two back to back conventions to go to, the first was in Edinburgh, Scotland, where the first England, Peter England, came from, and the second was in London, England. I remember getting my passport and trying to get the heavy dried scabs off my head so I would look halfway presentable for my passport photo. I didn't look good. Part of my head was still shaved, and I had this big dark bruise on my side from hitting the gear shifter in the crash.

My doctor examined me before the trip and saw something on my kidney, but he brushed it off and said, "It's from the car accident, it's a bruise, you don't have any symptoms of it being anything serious because no loss of appetite or weight loss. Go on your trip, and when you come back, we'll do some scans, by then the hematoma should be gone. You have nothing to worry about."

So I left for the conventions. Everything went well during my travels, and two weeks later when I got back home, I did the tests again, and the "bruise" was still there. My doctor still didn't seem concerned about it, but I said, "No offense, but I'm going to go to a specialist."

The specialist gave me a completely different diagnosis. He said, "Steve, unfortunately, what you have has nothing to do with the car accident, but the accident is the only way we found out about it."

Very calmly he explained that he had done over a hundred of these surgeries. There was a mass in my kidney that couldn't be biopsied because it would spread—but he was 99 percent sure that's what it was, and I had to get it out of there if I wanted to live. I went in on a Wednesday, and he scheduled me Friday for the surgery.

I had a decision to make. Do I listen to my GP who said it's just a bruise? Or do I listen to the specialist?

I went with the specialist's recommendation, and it turned out his pathology report was right. I had renal cell carcinoma. I'm really glad I trusted his judgment and experience, because other than the bruise, there was no indication that I had cancer. No sickness, no weight loss or loss of appetite, no blood in my urine, nothing. Other than feeling slightly under the weather—I thought it was a case of mono—I had zero symptoms.

The mass was large, and it was hard to get to. Back then, these types of surgeries were a lot more invasive than they are today. They had to basically cut me in half, go through my ribcage and deflate my lung so they could move it out of the way to get to my kidney. It was a very painful operation, and healing took a long time.

While I was in the hospital, some things happened. Before I tell you what happened, I'd like to preface this by mentioning that I was raised in a strict manner, sent to parochial school, and I spent my entire childhood under the rules and regulations of well-meaning, but very judgmental people. When I grew up and went out on my own, I was very successful in life. I thought that spiritual people were just using religion as a crutch, and that faith was a weakness. Being a strong person, I decided I didn't need it.

After the operation, many of my close friends and family came to see me, including a friend of mine, Larry and his wife. During their visit something they said triggered me. They basically told me I got cancer because I wasn't living for God, and that He did this to me as a wakeup call. It really rubbed me the wrong way. I got really angry and told them, "Get the hell out of my room! Leave and leave now—and don't bother coming back!"

What they said had only made things worse. I thought, *My grandfather died of kidney cancer, and here I'm sitting in this hospital bed, and they're judging me?!*

I couldn't get over it; it just felt so offensive to me.

Things changed after this.

One day I was walking up and down the halls of the hospital wing, listening to instrumental piano music on my headphones. I got to the end of the hallway where you could see out over the city. While I was standing there, looking out the window enjoying the view, something happened. God spoke to me. Very simply, like a father talking to a son with incredible love, he said, "Live for me."

And it completely melted me.

Standing there in the hospital hallway, weeping and alone, I made a decision. I just said, "Lord, I don't know if I have a week or a year to live, but I promise you, I'm going to give you my heart."

Today, I'm the same person, and I'm not perfect at all, but now the Lord is my absolute best friend. My heart has changed. I know what a hardened heart is because I used to have one. You can't hear the voice of God with a hardened heart. God could be warning you—just like my friend Larry said—but you can't hear it. You don't *want* to hear it. God didn't give me cancer, He allowed the accident to happen, to find the cancer and to give me a second chance, that is how much He loved me.

This experience changed me so much, my wife thought I'd gone completely crazy. When I came home from the hospital, I got rid of all my secular music and started listening to nothing but Christian music. I started going to church. My wife said (only half-jokingly), "Where is the man that I married?"

After my accident, I had more joy, peace, and fulfillment in that one year than in all the thirty-six years prior. I realized I wasn't happy all along. Even though I was financially successful, and I had a good marriage, I never felt truly "wealthy" because I wasn't balanced. My priorities weren't right. If you are not right with your Creator you will never be complete.

While I was recovering, I really had time to think about my priorities and ask myself what's important. I realized it's not really money and things—it's time. That changed my whole philosophy, how I talked to people, and how I looked at life. That's why I titled this chapter "There's More to Life Than Money."

It's all about the quality of life you're living.

This change of heart carried over into the work I was doing as a financial advisor.

Before this "wakeup call" I was always trying to close the sale, whether they were a fit for my services or not. Now, I make a point of only working with people who truly need my help, not just anybody. I focus on finding that one good client who really wants and needs my help, and by working with less people, it allows me to have a deeper relationship with the clients I have.

Before the accident, I would talk to clients about facts, assets, products, and rates of returns. Now, I talk about their hopes, and dreams, and plans. I ask them what they would like to accomplish in this lifetime, and whether they're living for themselves or for a child or grandchild.

You'd be amazed how many people I talk to who aren't fulfilled—money isn't everything!

If you can't sleep at night because your money is at risk, you need peace of mind. If you are miserable in your job, maybe it's time you find more fulfilling work, or just work less. It's all linked together. For me, I found balance with God. For them, it might be spending more time with family, or contributing more to society.

That's what the wealth lifestyle is all about, living the way you truly desire.

In my case, they caught the cancer early, I didn't have to do chemo or radiation, just the operation. Today, I live with one kidney, but I'm able to relatively live the same lifestyle as before. But I was very fortunate, I could have been paralyzed or had traumatic brain damage, and in my opinion, I was spared.

My wakeup call was drastic, but it doesn't have to be that way, you don't have to wait for a serious disaster to start making changes. If I learned one thing from this experience it was that people can change. That doesn't mean you quit your job tomorrow, but start putting together a plan for what you want to accomplish with the rest of your life. How much time do you have left, and what would you like to do with it? Having the income to accomplish that, that's true wealth.

Whether you believe me or not, it doesn't matter, because I'm not trying to convince you of anything. I didn't share my story with you to sell you anything. In the end, this message will reach who it's supposed to reach, and if it helps just one person, then it's all worth it.

In the next chapter, let's take a look at your priorities and see what your options are for developing a wealth lifestyle of your own.

CHAPTER 2

DEVELOPING THE WEALTH LIFESTYLE

When I met Pete, he was living in downtown Los Angeles working for a large national debt settlement company. The company was considered one of the best in the industry, but whenever he spoke about his work, Pete never seemed entirely satisfied.

One afternoon, I happened to be downtown and Pete showed me his office. The building was nice, but it was an absolute boiler room inside—all these guys packed into cubicles, cranking out phone calls, day after day. During lunch, Pete aired his complaints about the job—he was tired of fighting traffic every day, tired of being trapped in the office—ultimately, he'd be a lot happier if he could work remotely.

"Have you asked them if you can work from home?" I asked.

"Yes, but the company isn't set up for it."

Now I understood why Pete was less than enthusiastic about his career.

One day, Pete got a call from a headhunter who was looking to fill a spot at another top five company in the same space, and they were promising remote work. Pete took the job offer, but he didn't go 100 percent remote immediately, he started working from home at first, just a few days per week. Once he proved he could do that, he went into the office only one half a day per week, and then he took it a step further.

I got a call from Pete the other day, he just left Monaco and was boarding a flight to the Philippines. He sounded cheerful.

Today, Pete lives anywhere he wants in the world. As long as he has a computer and Wi-Fi, he's able to work. If he's in Europe, his costs might be the same, but in other places his costs are a lot less, like in the Philippines. He can live on much less money than he did in L.A. He's able to travel and live the lifestyle he wants, and his stress level is much lower. Turns out, not having to spend an hour each way in traffic every day was a complete game changer.

"What is true wealth? Obviously, it isn't just money."

This might be an extreme example, but the point I'm trying to make is it's all about lifestyle. Most people, like Pete, aren't totally thrilled where they're currently at. They've worked hard all their lives and they've been successful at accumulating assets, but now it's time for a much needed change. For him, the wealth lifestyle was the freedom to travel. For others, maybe just working from home a few days a week would be enough. Or commuting less. Or having more time to do things they want to do.

What is true wealth? Obviously, it isn't just money.

When I first started out in my career, I needed a job, so I went to work for an insurance company. Like most old school insurance agents, I spent my days on the phone. We'd go in to work on Sunday evenings, when people were home having dinner with their families, and we'd phone them up and try to set up appointments. All the agents had territories, you'd get your leads in the same area, and go out and knock on doors. Later, you'd get commissions on the sales. In other words, if you didn't hustle, you didn't eat.

One day, my office manager took me to a rural area in Maine to a town on Indian Island to visit a lead. That lead turned out to be a French Canadian man named Mr. Thibodaux, who lived upstairs in an apartment building he owned. We got into his place and sat down at his kitchen table, where the decisions are made. My manager was a "by the book" type of guy. He always told me, "Find out what they're worried about, and once you know their pain, you make the sale."

My manager stared across the table at the French Canadian, and said, "So ... Mr. T, what concerns you?"

That simple street smart man crossed his arms over his chest and said, "You. An insurance man sitting across the table from me, now that concerns me."

I've found that most people can read you like a book, so you have to be straight with them. Don't use a script or a canned game with them. I also learned that people I assumed would be good at sales, often weren't. Reading people and getting them to open up to you is a God given gift; some have it, and others don't.

Eventually, I got tired of the grind. One afternoon I went to see a lead, a nice older lady. When I got to talking with her, I found out she had Medicare supplements and she was on seven different plans trying to cover all her health care costs. It was illegal to sell someone more than one policy, because only one would pay, and she had seven. I decided I was done. I couldn't do it anymore. I found a new job that didn't require me to compromise my moral integrity, got my securities license, started investing, and eventually I started my own business as an advisor.

Sometimes when I think back on things I did when I was younger—working eighty hour weeks, going in on the weekends, spending all those hours on the road—I'm not sure how I ever did some of those things. When you get to my age (sixty-one at the moment), naturally you start to want to do more of the things you are able to enjoy, and less of the things you hate doing. And I'll go so far as to say, you've earned it.

Just like I transitioned out of the insurance business into financial advising, retirees are transitioning into the next phase of their lives. It's a natural progression. They're thinking about making some changes to their lifestyle, if they can, doing less of the things they dislike, and finding more time for family, or hobbies. Sometimes they can't change everything all at once, but most of the time they can do something differently, and start working toward their goals.

Developing the wealth lifestyle doesn't have to be radical, it's a process. Even just taking one step toward your joy, or away from something that steals your joy, can be life changing.

When I speak with clients, I would say 95 percent of people I meet aren't really happy with their lifestyle. So, I ask them, "What sort of change could you make that would make your life a lot more meaningful to you?"

They say, "Well, if I didn't have to be in this traffic every day," or, "If I didn't have to fly to China every other week," or, "The management's changed at my company, it's not what it used to be... If only I could do consulting instead."

Quality of life is part of a wealth lifestyle. So is having less stress.

In order to accomplish this, I tell them, "You need income. You need to have your bases covered."

Let me give you an example.

My friend Lee Carpenter is around fifty years old, and he's probably one of the hardest working guys I've ever met. Lee owns a commercial construction company, and every day he gets up at 3:30 am so he can arrive on site before the crews do. His company does around a million per year working on big water and sewer contracts for major cities in his area. The business is doing great, but the work takes a toll on Lee.

He was in perfect health his whole life, but one day he found this little lump on his neck, and his wife told him to get it checked out. It was melanoma. That was a wake-up call for him. There was no guarantee he could keep doing what he was doing forever.

Lee decided he wanted to have enough real estate so he would always have enough base income to cover his expenses. Every year, Lee bought a single family home and rented it out. Today, he owns sixteen total rental properties. He always said, "If I get hurt or I have to sell my company, I have enough coming in from my real estate."

Luckily, Lee's wife helps maintain the properties and run the business. He has everything he needs to pay his bills, and this gives him great peace of mind. He set himself up at a young age with a retirement plan, now if Lee wanted to quit working, or sell his company, or make a big lifestyle change, he's in a position to do so.

Another example is a friend of mine, a retired school principal. He bought a large parcel of land and turned it into a mobile home park. He rents the lots out, and it's a cash cow. The work is all done, and now he's retired and not only is it very valuable (mobile home parks sell easily), it generates a lot of income.

Another one is a retired law enforcement officer who invested in some hotels. He gets enough income from that, along with his pension, that it allows him to do other things with his investments, like take bigger risks. He can plan for more wealth transfer to his grandchildren, and make riskier investments with higher growth, because he doesn't need the income. The only reason he can do that is because he has that base set up.

No, real estate isn't for everyone. I understand that. There is a real downside to having to manage properties, and not everyone is cut out for it. The point I'm trying to make here is that these people have set up an income base. If you don't want real estate, then set something else up, so that you have a base for your wealth lifestyle.

> "What if your expenses were covered, and you had guaranteed income of $100,000 per year, for life? Now what would you do?"

If you're still working after all these years and you aren't able to stop doing what you're doing because of financial concerns—that's not the wealth lifestyle. That's why that income base is crucial.

Cover your expenses, that's the key. Once that's covered, you have the freedom to do other things, and take more risks, or do something outside the box.

That's why I always ask my clients, "What is your wealth lifestyle?"

What if your expenses were covered, and you had guaranteed income of $100,000 per year, for life? Now what would you do?

Would you work? Or would you take time off? Would you travel? Buy a home? Give it all to charity? What would make you happy? Is it sports cars, boats, and motorcycles? Or is it travel, scuba diving, and hiking?

While you ponder those questions, let's take a look at how retirement has changed in the modern era, and some of the real obstacles that can get in the way of you achieving the wealth lifestyle of your dreams. You may be surprised; they aren't what you think.

CHAPTER 3

RETIREMENT HAS CHANGED

In Junior High and High School, I was quite the accomplished track star. After winning the State and Regional Championship in the 100-yard dash, I won my first heat race which automatically qualified me for the finals at the Nationals. Even though my time wasn't the best, I went into the finals feeling super confident that I would win the whole thing. In my mind, there was no way I could lose.

The day of the finals I got out onto the track, there were eight of us on the line for the final and I ran the race of my life, it was my best time ever. But, one-by-one, I watched the other runners go whizzing by me. My feet were moving as fast and as hard as I possibly could, but they were just so much faster than me. By the end of the race, I finished sixth out of eight runners, I was crushed and humbled.

I did everything right, but I didn't even place ... not a good feeling.

Hard work and determination are crucial to success, but the big lesson I learned that day was that sometimes even when you do your best, you can still lose. It was somewhat deceiving by winning the first heat race so easily, because once I bumped up into the next level, I discovered so many guys were faster than me. Just when you think you are unbeatable, there is someone better than you. So, stay humble.

In my mind, this is very similar to the lesson Americans are learning right now about their retirement. Even though they're doing everything right—saving in their 401(k)s and IRAs, investing in mutual funds—it's not good enough. It feels like opportunities are passing them by. And they are.

The truth is: retirement has changed.

> "I know this is hard to hear, but your 'best' may not be good enough."

Thanks to inflation and currency devaluation, we're losing ground every day. You may have $100,000 in the bank, but it won't buy you as much as it did even just a few years ago. If you don't have your money in a financial vehicle that is designed to keep up with inflation, or if you put all your savings in the stock market and there's a downturn, you could still run out of money in retirement.

The point is, even if you're running the best race of your life, you could still lose. I know this is hard to hear, but your "best" may not be good enough.

Americans are doing what they think is right, only the game has changed. So, let's talk about what retirement looks like today in the modern age.

Retirement Doesn't Mean What It Used To

Retirement doesn't mean sitting on the couch watching football anymore. I like to compare retirement to owning a luxury sports car. You could park your car in your garage and never drive it again, but that would be the worst thing you could do to your car. It's the same with getting into shape. If you exercise and get fit, what good will it do to simply stop working out one day?

Retirement no longer means working for forty years straight, and then doing nothing at all. You may not have the same job you had before, you may be doing charity work, or working in a different capacity at the same job, or working from home, but the majority of retirees no longer stop working. They're still active, and working, they're just working differently.

Especially for men, their whole lives revolve around who they are and what they do for a living. If you suddenly take that away, even if we are okay financially, it doesn't do good things for our mental health. People need to stay active mentally and physically to be enthusiastic about their lives. The retirees I see who are doing the best, and have the least health issues, are the ones who are staying busy, putting themselves to good use for others.

For instance, there was a woman I knew named Ruby who worked for a major drug company for twenty-five years. She saved a considerable amount of money, and along with her partial pension and social security, she was able to retire comfortably and take care of her husband. After her husband passed from cancer, Ruby decided to devote her time to Meals on Wheels. Between her charity work, church, friends, and family, Ruby is quite active. This is someone who isn't sitting around doing nothing. And thanks to her smart retirement planning, she had the guaranteed income to allow her the time to give back to her community.

Another example is Harold, a former associate of mine. He worked in the corporate world his whole life and hated the stress. When he retired, he decided to do Christian talk radio, and travel. In between recording shows for his radio ministry and the mission work he does in Ukraine a few times a year, he also cares for his parents who are in their 90s and he takes care of his daughter's dogs. Between family, radio, and mission work—Harold is busy. He's set himself up with guaranteed income, and his needs are taken care of, so he's able to do what he wants. His stress levels have gone way down, and he loves his lifestyle.

> "I wouldn't even call it retirement anymore. It's your new lifestyle, and for some, it's the next phase of your working life."

My brother was a firefighter for many years, and he retired without much of a pension. To offset that, he flips houses and sells real estate on the side and has managed to make enough from those deals for him and his wife to live comfortably in retirement. He retired at a relatively young age, so he and his wife have an active lifestyle. He's always got a real estate project he's working on, but he's happy, stress free, and healthy. This is a sharp contrast to the taxing work he did for the fire department working on the ambulance team as an EMT and firefighter.

I wouldn't even call it retirement anymore. It's your new lifestyle, and for some, it's the next phase of your working life. Everyone is different but putting yourself in a financial position to do more of the things you love—that's the goal.

Given that you're not stopping, but only shifting your priorities, what you really want are options in retirement. Because once you have income and options, you have control over your own destiny.

Unfortunately, we're stuck with the word retirement for now, even though the term has become obsolete. Speaking of obsolete things, the definition of retirement isn't the only thing that's changed in recent years.

Without realizing it, many Americans are using old tools, old information, that no longer applies to our current situation. Let's go over some of these things.

Disappearing Pensions

According to a recent article from online magazine *the balance* titled "The History of the Pension Plan" by Melissa Phipps, up until the early 1980s, most people had pensions. Because of this, many companies began looking for a way to wiggle out of their commitment. I assume they were afraid if everyone retired all at once, they wouldn't be able to pay the pensions. What came next were defined contribution plans such as 401(k), 403(b), and 457 plans, where the employee would make the bulk of the contribution to the plan, and the employer may or may not match a portion of those contributions. Over the next few decades, contribution plans rapidly outpaced pensions in popularity.

As a result, today many people in their 60s have 80-90 percent of their savings in a 401(k) or similar retirement savings plan, and nothing in their pensions. When it comes to retirement, the only thing that matters is guaranteed income, so right there, we know if something happens to the market, that your 401(k) is at risk.

The shift from pensions to contribution plans happened so quickly that many Americans have gone off kilter with their retirement strategy, without realizing it. They're so focused on making money and saving it in their 401(k), that by the time they retire, a single market correction could throw their entire plan off.

Increased Risk

Without guaranteed income, just hoping the markets will generate enough money for you to live on for the rest of your life—is high risk. And yet, if you ask most people, that's exactly what they're doing.

When it comes to retirement, there are both known and unknown risks. Inflation and deflation are a risk. Market losses are a risk. Longevity is a risk. So are taxes, long term care, and health care. All these factors hurt your money and put stress on your retirement, instead of helping you.

Without guaranteed income, anything could happen. Not only do we have 401(k)s instead of pensions, today we have hedge funds, ETFs, and all sorts of risky investment strategies in the marketplace. You used to be able to buy quality stock—not so much anymore. Compounding this, people are living longer than ever today, and health care or long term care expenses have to be factored in.

Take a look at the chart below, for example. Who could have predicted this? One person runs out of money, and the other is okay. All because they didn't have a retirement plan that accounted for the risk and accurately predicted a sequence of returns. This goes to show that seemingly minor mistakes in your planning can yield disastrous results.

Sequence of Returns

Valued Client, age 60, North Carolina
Initial Balance: **$ 1,000,000**
Withdrawal Rate: **7.00%**
Gains captured: **75%**

Year	Beginning Balance, $	Historical Return, %	Annual Withdrawal, $	Beginning Balance, $	Historical Return, %	Annual Withdrawal, $
2000	1,000,000	-10.1	70,000	1,000,000	0.0	70,000
2001	828,608	-13.0	70,000	930,000	0.0	70,000
2002	650,535	-23.4	70,000	860,000	0.0	70,000
2003	428,531	26.4	70,000	790,000	19.8	70,000
2004	471,580	9.0	70,000	876,304	6.7	70,000
2005	443,991	3.0	70,000	865,411	2.3	70,000
2006	387,315	13.6	70,000	814,890	10.2	70,000
2007	370,066	3.5	70,000	828,127	2.6	70,000
2008	313,127	-38.5	70,000	780,049	0.0	70,000
2009	122,618	23.5	70,000	710,049	17.6	70,000
2010	81,377	12.8	70,000	764,952	9.6	70,000
2011	21,779	0.0	21,778	768,288	0.0	70,000
2012	0	13.4	0	698,288	10.1	70,000
2013	0	29.6	0	698,495	22.2	70,000
2014	0	11.4	0	783,568	8.5	70,000
2015	0	-0.7	0	780,508	0.0	70,000
2016	0	9.5	0	710,508	7.2	70,000
2017	0	19.4	0	691,318	14.6	70,000
2018	0	-6.2	0	722,008	0.0	70,000
Total	0	3.0	791,778	652,008	6.0	1,330,000

So many people aren't set up correctly for retirement, they desperately need a plan that factors in risk and is focused on security, and instead they are just winging it.

Social Security

When I talk with clients, I often hear questions like, "I'm sixty-two, do I retire now, or do I wait and get more?" "Can I rely on social security?" "Will it still be there when I retire?"

The truth is, there is a lot of uncertainty surrounding social security benefits. At the rate government spending and our national debt is increasing, there's good cause for being concerned. It's great that we have social security in this country, but my guess is it's not going to last forever. This calls for some additional income planning, just in case.

Rising Costs

Every time we go to the grocery store, we notice the prices are going up. The truth is: our money doesn't go as far as it used to.

To stay competitive in the world, the United States has had to devalue our currency. This creates inflation and rising costs of living that become more noticeable as we age. This is especially hard for people in retirement, as they are on a fixed income, and their purchasing power is disappearing right under their noses. Nobody can seem to afford vehicles or homes these days without relying on credit lines.

As a result, there's been a sharp increase in debt among older Americans, struggling to pay off their credit cards and mortgages.

According to a recent CNBC article by Annie Nova, "Growing Debt Among Older Americans Threatens Their Retirement," in the past decade, there's been a steep increase in debt among households headed by someone age 75 and older. Debt in the form of mortgages, credit cards and even student loans in addition to inflation have become a huge part of the retirement landscape, and that is proving difficult for most Americans to adjust to when considering their quality of life in retirement.

New Old Tools

The good news is, not all the changes have been bad.

There are new financial products on the market that can offset some of the risks I just laid out. Most of these are actually old tools, such as annuities and cash value life insurance policies, that have been refurbished so they're more attractive to consumers. Improvements such as reduced or zero fees, and hybrid products that serve multiple purposes. For instance, in the past, you used to have to give the government a huge chunk of your money just to withdraw your income in retirement. These days you can have a rider on your retirement account, and with a small fee, you will have guaranteed lifetime income.

Once you've identified the risks, there are a variety of solutions in our financial marketplace today that will cover your needs. In my opinion, there's no comparison between the old products of yesteryear, and the new and improved ones.

The only thing you want to be aware of is these products are often complicated to set up, and most advisors haven't been in the business long enough to have the experience necessary. Don't let your neighborhood banker try to set up a complicated financial product for you. It can make a huge difference in your money, how the legal contract is designed, and which product you pick for your personalized retirement strategy.

So, don't do it without help!

Think of It as Setting Up Your Own Pension

Today, most companies outside the federal government don't have pensions. And even those workers that do have pensions, aren't always guaranteed to receive them. What if your company goes out of business? Or the state you're in has gone bankrupt? Your actual pension could go down the drain.

But if you set something up yourself—a self-directed pension—you can be assured that it's there for you when you need it the most.

It's not all about money, it's your lifestyle.

You've worked hard all your life, what are you doing this for? Hopefully, so you can live the way you want to live and enjoy yourself. You want a fulfilling end of your life. So, keep in mind, you can run the race and still lose. In the next chapter, we'll be talking about covering your bases, and how to figure out how much income you'll actually need in retirement.

CHAPTER 4

COVERING YOUR BASES

In 1983, I had just started out as an insurance broker, and then received my 6 & 63 securities licenses, and sold mutual funds and variable annuities. I was young and ambitious, in my twenties, working hard to make my way up the ladder. By 1986, I was full tilt, I had earned myself a reputation as one of the best in the industry and was winning awards. Then, Black Monday happened. For those of you too young to remember, it was the single largest drop in the market since the Great Depression.

I'm a relationship driven person by nature, so I've always made a point of being close with my clients. It was devastating. All these people had trusted me, friends, family, even my own parents, and all I could do was stand by helplessly as their assets dropped in half. I didn't know what to do. I was taught we had to go and hold their hand and tell them things would come back, to be patient. When things didn't come back right away, people started to panic.

Before Black Monday, my clients were making great returns. I was selling mutual funds like Putnam Health Sciences Trust and clients were making 30 percent or more every year. I always say, a broker is like a weatherman, you're a God in a way, when things are going well, you're the man. People are making money, and everybody is happy. But when things go the other way .... watch out! You're the one they're going to blame.

Because I'd been focused so heavily on growth and high yield returns, I overlooked one of the most important factors—safety. Painfully, I began to see the importance of having a mix of low risk and higher risk strategies working simultaneously, with an emphasis on guaranteed income that wasn't subject to market fluctuations, taxation, or fees. In other words, making sure my clients had their bases covered, no matter what.

I began looking for safer products to get my clients into, and I was so excited when the first fixed index annuity products came out. The idea that people would have safety of principle and still have potential gains from the market index, I just loved the concept. I noticed most of my clients were close to retirement, already retired, or retiring soon. They couldn't afford to take the type of risks they might have desired when they were younger. These types of clients needed safer—more boring—investment vehicles, and fixed annuities fit the bill nicely. The most important thing to help them maintain their lifestyle in retirement was making sure they had guaranteed income for life, and that they're bases were covered. That was it.

With that, I moved most of my client's assets into fixed index products, so their principle would be protected. I sold some of the first indexed products that came out on the market. I held on to all the statements and kept a close watch on them in the months following the stock market collapse. Lo and behold, soon enough my clients were making 24-28 percent return on their money and loving it.

I did not want my friends, family, or clients to ever lose money on my watch again; I was embarrassed and felt responsible. Never again would there be another Black Monday. By the time the 2008 "Great Recession" hit, I had hundreds of clients, but this time around none of them lost money. The worst that could happen is that they weren't making a lot of returns during the downturn, but they certainly weren't losing money either. This gave me great peace of mind.

Today, this philosophy of "covering your bases" has carried so far into my practice that setting up cash flow in the form of guaranteed income is the first thing I do for my clients. In fact, I'm proud to say it's something I did for the person I so loved and brought me into this world, my Mother.

Shortly after Black Monday, my mother decided to retire. She had a little bit of savings left from her job as a bank teller and a 401(k) and she asked me what she should do with it. It wasn't a lot of money, but the last thing I wanted was to be talking to my mother about money during our visits. I told her I didn't want to handle it, but she insisted. So, I went to my mentor Robbie Robinson, a broker of forty years, dad of Todd Robinson who founded LPL Financial and trained me, to ask for advice.

I said to Robby, "I don't know what product to put her money into."

I'll never forget what he told me: "Steve, pick something she would want. It has to 'fit' your mother, not what you think is best or would pick for yourself."

It was great advice. Robby told me to find out how clients feel about risk and returns and then figure out what income they'll need to cover their bases and fit them into the program that works best for them. My mother, it turned out, was a fixed rate kind of a girl. She didn't like a lot of risk. She had mutual funds in the past, but she didn't like to lose any amount of money, no matter how insignificant.

I put her with a company which is Fortis now, USG back then, in a fixed rate program, and she stayed with that company for the rest of her life. It paid better interest than bank rates, automatically renewed every year, and it was steady, and that fit my mother perfectly. My mother took the interest from that account and used it to cover her basic expenses in her retirement. She had nothing to complain about, and it was all because of Robby's good advice. Luckily, I listened to him, because I was still young back then and I probably would have picked something more aggressive, and she wouldn't have liked it.

I'll never forget, at the end of my mother's life she was more focused on the afterlife than anything else. Even though she was terminally ill, she made sure I knew she was happy with that account. It fit her like a glove, and it gave her the comfort and peace of mind she needed in retirement. On her deathbed, she told me, "I was always really happy about that."

It was really sweet to hear those words, and to know that I was able to give my mother a retirement without financial stress. Since then, I have used Robbie's advice with all my clients all throughout my career.

> "Until you have your bases covered, you shouldn't be risking more than you can afford to lose."

No program is perfect, they all have limitations, but the best I can do is to fit them into the product that works for them and covers their bases. Turns out, most people are as happy as they can be with that. Some people have financial products like contribution plans or cash value life insurance policies, or they put money into a guaranteed annuity, and others have pensions and social security, or they accumulate assets to make up the differences. But either way, I make sure they have their bases covered first.

That's what we're talking about. Covering your fixed bases, creating a plan for when you retire or semi-retire, and then later, when you have your bases covered you can go invest in things with more risk. Until you have your bases covered, you shouldn't be risking more than you can afford to lose.

Cash Flow is Financial Freedom

I was talking with several friends of mine the other day, one is a CPA, one is an event planner, and one works for Energizer. Every one of them said the same thing, "I don't know how much longer I can do this." Even the CPA, who technically owns his own firm, said he's not planning on doing his job for more than a couple more years.

I've noticed a definite trend, once people get a certain number of assets, they start thinking about freedom more than money. They start reassessing their lifestyle and dreaming about what they really wish they were doing instead. They have choices now, and they start weighing their options.

I'd say 80 percent of the people I talk to at that age are looking for a change. By late 60s, they're going to make some changes; it's the norm, and I've come to expect it. Still, it's amazing the stories you hear.

I had a client who came to my office the other day, and she said, "I'm not going to live with that man in my retirement!"

I was startled by her tone of voice. "Who?" I asked.

"My husband," she said. "We've had problems for years. I need to make sure I have enough if we're not together."

She wasn't sure it was over, but just in case, she wanted enough income to support herself in his absence. It gave her financial peace of mind, that's what we're talking about. Covering your bases with guaranteed income.

Her story is an unusual case, and they've since worked things out, but regardless, she's now set up so that if she's with her husband or not, she can live comfortably. She has cash flow, and financial freedom. Even if you're in a great marriage, covering your bases is important. You have to think about the surviving spouse and whether you're both independently set up with income for retirement.

Even though the details are a bit different, many people tell similar stories. They're looking for the wealth lifestyle—having a little more of what they like, and less of what they don't. The majority of people I talk to are successful, they've paid their dues, and made some money. They're ready to make some adjustments to their lifestyle. And the key to this is income: cash flow is financial freedom.

Now that we've covered that, let's talk about some of the things that can get in the way of your wealth lifestyle, such as taking too much risk with your money, having assets that are too difficult to manage (like too many rental properties), taxes, and dealing with the challenges of getting older, such as health issues and longevity. In the next chapter, we'll be taking a look at what I call tax free retirement—in my opinion it's one of the major keys to achieving a wealth lifestyle—but before we do that, I'd like you to ponder some questions that will help you assess where you're currently at: What would you do if you had $16,000 guaranteed income each month? What do you wish you could change about your lifestyle? Are your bases covered? If they aren't, then how much money do you think you need to retire, or semi-retire? (Some can live on $25,000 a year and others can't live on anything less than $100,000). And finally, do you have financial peace of mind?

CHAPTER 5

TAX FREE RETIREMENT

The last time you spoke with your financial advisor, how much tax free retirement income did they tell you you'd have in your portfolio? This is a loaded question, by the way, nobody has sat down with their advisor and determined tax free income, because no one in my industry does this. In fact, 99 percent of people I've asked this say their advisor hasn't even mentioned it.

Maybe it hasn't even occurred to you that there is tax free income in retirement to be had. After all, nobody talks about, it's like the elephant in the room.

> "In my opinion, this should be one of the first things you ask your advisor: 'How do I get more tax free income in retirement?'"

Nowadays, people are willing to go to drastic measures to reduce the amount they have to pay the federal government every year in taxes. If you can move to a different state and save $25,000 a year in taxes—why not do it? That's a decision lots of people are willing to make. I've known so many people who relocated to take advantage of low, or no, income tax. I even had a friend who moved to Tennessee to escape the draconian state taxes he was paying in California. This isn't uncommon. So, if taxes are such a big deal, why aren't we talking about tax free retirement income?

In my opinion, this should be one of the first things you ask your advisor: "How do I get more tax free income in retirement?" Some people don't mind paying income taxes as long as they have more income, and others want the maximum tax free benefits— either way, we should be talking about it.

Creating a tax free retirement might be harder to do if you're trying to retire this year, but if you have five or more years before retirement, it's really simple to create a bucket of tax free income. So, how can you accomplish this? There are several tried and true methods, and they include tax free bonds, Roth IRAs, and properly structured Indexed Universal Life insurance policies. Let's look at some case studies from clients I've worked with, to give you a better idea of what setting up a tax free retirement looks like in real life.

There was a retired dentist from North Carolina who became a client of mine, and he was one of the rare ones. He already had some tax free income in a life insurance policy, but he simply wanted me to re-evaluate his policy and his strategy. In the end, we found him a better indexed product to move his money into. With the remainder of the money, he set up a charitable trust through a non-profit group in New York. Later, we rolled even more of his money into a Fixed Index Universal Life Insurance policy. Today, he has the best "tax shelter" you can find, and in addition to his investments, he's set for life with a tax free retirement plan. He's also become our biggest "tax free retirement" cheerleader.

I mentioned my friend who works for Energizer in the last chapter. He just did a million dollar 401(k) rollover, but he's got another ten years before retirement. He asked me to set him up with something that would give him tax free income, and also provide long term health care. I proposed a cash value life insurance policy to add to his portfolio. At first, he wasn't sure, but his wife liked the plan, and they both took out policies on each other, with the goal of putting enough in them over the next five to seven years to gain the maximum benefits from them. In this case, the key here is to not over-fund the policies all at once, so that it still works for them, but doesn't get them into trouble with the IRS.

Another client of mine is a CPA, who was working high up in the IRS before he started his own private accounting practice. He has big clients, including major hoteliers, and other large international corporations. This man was extremely financially cautious and conservative, but he came to me because he was having some issues with the trust he'd set up, and his life insurance policy. First, I referred him to an excellent tax attorney, who straightened out his trust. Then, I evaluated his life insurance policy. We were able to get him into a different policy, an Indexed Universal Life, with the same overall structure, but $500,000 more for his family. He made an extra $500,000 tax free; that's a huge gain! Since then, he's referred us to many of his clients, friends, and family members, including his son who just applied for his own policy.

As you can see, my main area of expertise is life insurance policies, and I prefer it largely because of the versatility of the product. But there is also one more important reason why life insurance outperforms all the others: health care.

Health is Wealth

Most people I talk to have health insurance, but if they ever had a serious health crisis, or needed long term care—they aren't covered. The reality is, over half of all bankruptcies filed in America are tied to medical expenses—either because of the costs or because of time out of work. According to CNBC writer Lorie Konish in a recent article titled "This is the Real Reason Most Americans File for Bankruptcy," an estimated 530,000 families file for bankruptcy each year because of medical expenses.

The chances of you having a major illness increases exponentially as you get older. If you get sick in retirement, and you don't qualify for Medicaid, suddenly you could be paying $9,000 a month for long term care. I've seen this happen. I had a friend who retired with a nice sum of money just shy of one million dollars. Toward the end of his life, he went into a nursing home and within a few years he'd spent all his savings. There was nothing left to pass on to his children. In some ways, it's even worse than dying.

Major medical insurance doesn't cover every scenario a lot of times. Even if you do have long term care in your plan, you may not be covered for long term cost, or home care. If you have a car accident or a stroke, you might be covered for a short while, but after so many days you won't be covered at all. One major health problem, and you could go through your entire life's savings in a matter of months.

Life insurance can fill in the gap that medical coverage doesn't address, as well as provide tax free income, and a traditional death benefit. If you die before you've completed your plan, your family receives the benefit tax free, and often it's much more money than you've put into it. If you don't die, but you are permanently injured or disabled to the point where you can't perform daily activities, you can accelerate the policy and use a percentage of the death benefit for living expenses, up to $10,000 per month—and yes, it's tax free.

How can it be tax free? This is how it works, when you withdraw money from your life insurance policy you are technically loaning the money to yourself, and loans aren't taxable. You can take your money out of a life insurance policy without having to pay income taxes on it, and it's perfectly legal to do so. Also, when money is given to your beneficiary from the life insurance policy in the form of a death benefit, this is also tax free.

> "In my opinion, Indexed Universal Life insurance is the 'Swiss Army Knife' of financial products."

It's not for everybody, though, and you do go through an underwriting process to determine whether you're eligible. It may make sense for your situation or it may not. This is why I try to carefully evaluate my clients to make sure it's a good fit before I recommend it.

In my opinion, Indexed Universal Life insurance is the "Swiss Army Knife" of financial products. It solves a multitude of problems including critical health issues and long term care costs, which are the biggest blind spot in retirement planning currently.

So, why aren't more people using them?

Some may be turned off by the concept of life insurance, even if they agree with the tax and death benefits, there is something about life insurance that they find distasteful. Some have had bad past experiences with unscrupulous or incompetent insurance agents, and as a result, aren't receptive to it. Lastly, not everyone is eligible, especially if they aren't in good health. Out of ten clients, I probably propose life insurance policies to one or two of them, and the rest it doesn't fit their situation, they don't qualify, or they're just not interested. Like I said, it isn't for everybody, but it's an option.

Who does it work well for? It works well for those looking to create tax free income; it works well for people who want a retirement savings account that isn't subject to the whims of the stock market or government regulation; it works well as a way to cover costs for major health crises, disability, and long term care; and it also works for people looking to provide a benefit for their family and heirs when they die. Life insurance is just one slice of your retirement "pie," to help you cover your bases, and fund your wealth lifestyle. In my opinion, it's a vehicle with pros and cons, just like annuities, stocks, bonds, social security, contribution plans, IRAs, and pensions. At the end of the day, what you want an advisor to do is tailor your portfolio specifically to meet your needs—whether that's with life insurance or not.

So, if your advisor isn't addressing the elephant in the room, next time you should ask them, "How can I get more tax free income in retirement?"

If they are truly worth their salt, they'll have an answer for that as well as a plethora of strategies and products to recommend to you, with the goal of helping you get the most out of your retirement. From what I've seen, all good advisors have a system, a patented step-by-step process that they take their clients through. I call mine the Wealth Lifestyle Method, and we'll be discussing this in greater detail in the following chapters.

CHAPTER 6

THE WEALTH LIFESTYLE METHOD

When Robert came to me, he was in his early sixties, working for a large company, and just starting to think about retirement. Last year, his company was bought by a much larger firm, and now there was new management with a lot of pressure being put on the employees that carried over from the former ownership—it seemed like a good time for Robert to get out of the corporate world.

As for retirement planning, Robert was given a standard 401(k) with company matching, and a pension, which was relatively small. Like most of my clients, Robert couldn't see himself stopping working entirely, but he was wondering if he could consult, work less, or maybe start a business of his own. His career wasn't in any danger, but he was fed up. As his wife Martha put it, "He's counting the days."

During our assessment, my first priority was listening to Robert and Martha talk about their current life, their finances, and their frustrations. When they had finished explaining their situation in great detail, they asked me things like, "How much income will we need to retire?"

"Can I take this out of my savings?" "Will we have enough money?"

If I was like most advisors, I would have jumped right into planning. Started talking about different financial strategies and laying out the numbers. Not me. I like to talk to people. In fact, I've had clients tell me during our meetings they feel like they're talking to a psychiatrist! I want them to tell me everything—their hopes, their dreams, what their goals are, how they feel about taking risks. Who are they? What keeps them up at night? I'm not a life coach or a counselor, but I'm more than happy to listen to my clients because it helps me do a better job for them. I get excited when my clients are excited about their life, naturally.

I began asking Bob and Martha to talk about their dreams with me. Do you like taking family vacations? Where do your kids live? Do you want more time with your family? Could you see yourself becoming a consultant? Do you want a vacation home?

As they were talking, I began drawing a diagram on the notepad on my desk. It had two columns, Left and Right. On the Left side was the current state of things, their jobs, their assets, and their savings. On the Right side column, was a list of the things that they'd mentioned were important to them, like more free time, autonomy, peace of mind, and financial security.

I held up the notepad for Bob and Martha to see. "See this? Point A to point B. Now, how do we get you from here to there?"

> "How do you plan for a future without a vision of what that'll look like? It's not possible."

Over my years as an advisor, I've found that many of my clients are in a similar situation as Bob and Martha—they're ready for a big change. They've had enough of the corporate grind. They want out. But what do they really want to do instead? Ultimately, what does their future look like? Oftentimes, they don't know. They're unhappy, but they haven't really figured out what the alternative looks like.

How do you plan for a future without a vision of what that'll look like? It's not possible.

That's why the first step in the Wealth Lifestyle Method is identifying where you are today, assessing your current finances, and talking about how you feel about your life. Secondly, we find out where you want to be. What your wealth lifestyle looks like. This is a proven method, an assessment process that helps to match my client's preferences with their retirement plans. I talk about their dreams and develop a vision of where they want to go—their future.

After all, what good is planning, if you don't know what your preferences are?

Wealth is a lifestyle, not a number. If you're chronically worried and stressed day to day, panicking over money or miserable, dying to get out of your job—you aren't living a wealthy lifestyle. Peace of mind is true wealth.

Most people just need to make some adjustments, but which changes you make, makes all the difference in the world.

For instance, maybe you want to retire and live in Mexico City. Well, if that's what you want to do, my goal is to get you there! How do I help you achieve that? Most people just want more peace of mind and control over their workday. Naturally, as you get older, you can't work as hard as you did when you were younger. You tire out easier, or you may have health issues that cause you to slow down a bit. Things change. You may have grandchildren in college, or aging parents to look after, properties to manage, and more responsibilities. The point is, my job is to find out what you are really looking to do, and then figure out a way to help you achieve that.

The idea is to get the things the way you want, the way you want them, not what your advisor wants—that's the key. Most advisors tell you what to do with your money, the Wealth Lifestyle Method is not about that. This is about getting you closer to the lifestyle you have always dreamed of living.

I can't tell you how many times I've sat down with clients and discovered their retirement planning was totally off kilter. Sometimes I test them by giving them loaded questions like, "Do you want your money insured, or at risk?" or, "Do you want to pay taxes now, or later, when they're higher?" or, "Do you want to pay more fees?"

I already know the answers to these questions, but I want them to hear themselves saying it out loud. Eventually, they come to the conclusion on their own that their current plan doesn't match up with what they need. There is a discrepancy between what they said they wanted, and what they had. Nothing is perfect, and no retirement plan is foolproof, but the reality is that these people aren't set up for living a wealth lifestyle. Somebody had sold them a product that wasn't a great fit for them.

> "You're counting the days on the calendar until your retirement. You're daydreaming about a change of pace, doing something more fulfilling with your time, having more freedom. You are ready for a change."

You may feel completely stuck in your current situation. You're burned out. Even though you make good money, you can't remember the last time you felt enthusiastic about your career. You dread going in to work at the office. You're counting the days on the calendar until your retirement. You're daydreaming about a change of pace, doing something more fulfilling with your time, having more freedom. You are ready for a change.

Instead of sitting around complaining, it's time to start planning. You know where you're at right now—where do you really want to be?

There are several key components to the Wealth Lifestyle Method: creating a vision, overhead, income streams, protection from taxes, reducing risks, and leaving a wealth legacy. In the remaining chapters of this book, we're going to examine the process step-by-step, starting with overhead, which in my opinion is the first major obstacle preventing you from achieving your wealth lifestyle. Don't forget about our case study with Robert and Martha, we're going to continue to follow their journey through the entire system, so you can see for yourself whether it paid off in the end.

CHAPTER 7

WHAT'S STOPPING YOU?

When I was in my twenties, all my liquid cash was tied up in commercial real estate and without realizing it, I had over-leveraged my business. When the real estate market crashed in the late 1980s, I went down with it. There was nothing left to do, I had to file for bankruptcy.

At the time, I was in the middle of building a new home and a car dealership, and now both were just sitting there half-finished on the lots. I had contractors after me, some I had known all my life—I couldn't pay any of them. People around town were talking behind my back. On top of this, one of the neighbors near the car dealership had publicly accused us of disturbing a creek nearby with our construction build and doing work in a flood zone without proper permits. Nothing could move forward until after we had it out with her in the City Council meeting. My workers were angry, my family was upset, and now my neighbors hated me.

Overall, I just felt like such a loser. Here I was, nearly thirty years old, starting all over again.

Luckily, I had been raised to work hard all my life. Even from an early age, I was always expected to work and earn money to pay for school clothes, bicycles, and toys. My parents taught me well, and I tapped into that work ethic and somehow pulled myself out of the financial ditch I had fallen into. We eventually got the properties finished, but all in all, it was a horrible experience.

Despite the trauma and humiliation of this experience, during this time I learned the most valuable financial lesson of all: the importance of overhead.

I had committed the cardinal sin of not making sure there was enough cash flow to cover my bases. Ignoring my expenses, I sank everything I had into real estate, assuming money would be coming in shortly from my investments, and I left myself, my family, and my lifestyle unprotected.

> "Imagine your retirement as a faraway destination, and income is the gas you put into your vehicle to get you there."

Now that you have your vision of the retirement lifestyle you want, the most crucial step in the Wealth Lifestyle Method is figuring out the bare bones costs—in other words, your overhead. Imagine your retirement as a faraway destination, and income is the gas you put into your vehicle to get you there. Without enough gas, you're likely to stall out somewhere along the way, and wind up stranded by the side of the road. Assessing your needs and coming up with a list of total expenses is absolutely essential.

What is the bare minimum you need to survive? How much income will it take to get you where you want to be?

What's Stopping You?

It could be fear. It could be procrastination. It could be that you and your spouse are on a different page. But for most people, the single biggest thing stopping them from attaining their Wealth Lifestyle is money.

My clients Robert and Martha were no exception.

Robert's son lived a few states away in Florida, and he had a couple kids of his own. Not only was Robert unhappy at work, he also didn't get to see his grandchildren all that much. Robert and Martha had a big house on a lake, but it was cold and icy where they lived, and the long winters were becoming intolerable. On top of this, Martha was dealing with some minor health issues, and they both felt it would be better to be closer to their son and grandchildren in Florida so they could help out, with the added benefit of being in a warmer climate.

Robert and Martha were the quintessential empty nesters. They owned a large lakeside home, about 5,000 square feet, worth $800,000 dollars, and they owed very little on it. The location was ideal when they were younger, but now that they were older, Robert and Martha didn't go out on the lake anymore. Their home had a lot of value, but their money was completely tied up in it. Not to mention, it was too big of a house for just the two of them

At first, Robert considered working remotely, thinking maybe that would solve the problem. "Maybe I could become a consultant," he said during our meeting.

When we assessed Robert and Martha's financial situation and came up with a total overhead cost, it was clear to me that they needed to make some big decisions in the next few years that would take cash above and beyond their daily expenses. Becoming a consultant might help solve some of the problems, but it wouldn't generate nearly enough income to give them the real boost forward they needed.

As it stood, they didn't have enough liquid assets to make the kinds of changes I foresaw them making in the next few years. I didn't want to come right out and tell them to sell the home, but I knew if they took the value of that property and sold it, it would give them the cash they needed to free themselves from their situation.

I believe that honesty really is the best policy. As they were telling me more about their current financial situation, I casually said, "Have you considered buying a cheaper house in Florida somewhere off the water for $300,000?"

That caught their attention.

I continued. "You'd have $400,000 left over to do retirement planning with."

Robert and Martha were blown away; they hadn't even considered selling their lake home.

In the end, we created an income plan based around the sale of their house. They had enough liquid cash left over from that sale to fund a relocation closer to their children, without risking or sacrificing their quality of life. From there, Robert was left with the much easier decision of whether to keep his job as a remote consultant or retire completely.

Not everyone is willing to make such a major change right away, everyone's appetite for risk looks a bit different. Some people stay in their homes until the absolute last minute and it's time to move to a retirement community, where all they have to do is pay rent. Some are empty nesters and they move because they don't need all the extra space now that they're kids are grown. And some would prefer slightly different living situations, for instance if the home is two stories and they're not able to climb as many stairs as when they were younger.

Whatever the motivation, retirement planning sometimes involves difficult decisions such as downsizing, relocation, or getting the entire family on board with your plan. It may not happen overnight. You may have to compromise with your partner, or even adjust your own goals in order to get where you're going. But the first big obstacle is overhead. Once you have that exact number in mind, it's so much easier to create an income plan that both covers your bases, and gives you the freedom to make major changes, if necessary.

Similarly, clients come to me with various degrees of preparedness. Some have been stockpiling assets, investing in rental properties, or setting up multiple income streams. Others are just getting started building a guaranteed income. The point is, how do we use the lifestyle you've already created to live the life you want?

Now that we've addressed basic costs of living and what it takes to fund your wealth lifestyle, let's talk about another important issue for retirement planning: protecting your money.

CHAPTER 8

PROTECTING YOUR ASSETS

Sometimes planning for the future of retirement feels like swimming with the alligators.

In order to maintain a wealth lifestyle, you'll need to be protected from all sides, and that's why I like to create a "money shield" around my clients' assets. This "money shield" accounts for and mitigates every type of risk your money will face in retirement: taxes, inflation, long term care, health care, market volatility and so on.

A true wealth lifestyle protects your money, but also gives you peace of mind.

When I work with clients like Robert and Martha, I worry that they're not protected enough. People who are super wealthy don't have to worry about these things so much—they have millions—but middle class and upper middle class Americans generally have to deal with a lot of risks. They've accumulated enough assets to be wealthy, but they still have to worry about making one false move that could send it all toppling.

There has been a historical increase in risk to our wealth over the years, not a decrease, so keep this in mind—charting a safe and financially secure path forward into retirement isn't getting any easier. Some of these risks may seem minor, but they can make a much bigger difference for someone in retirement, as there is generally a lot less time to recover from financial setbacks. If you're over sixty, no more than 40 percent of your total assets should be at risk, because a loss of assets could be a real problem when you're trying to generate income and cover your bases at the same time.

Exploring some of the biggest dangers and risks associated with retirement is one of the first things I do with my clients.

Long Term Care

Robert and Martha were sitting across from my desk in my office. We had come to the point in our assessment meeting where I needed to talk about some of the more difficult challenges of their retirement plan.

"I know this is pretty far in the future ... but have you put any thought into long term care?" I asked them.

The husband and wife exchanged looks.

"No, we hadn't really thought about it," Martha said.

"Long term care could cost you," I said. "Let me tell you why."

I continued. "I knew a gentleman by the name of Norman, who had a great job, a very high profile position with FEMA. Norman was good at saving his money and when he was ready to retire, he had about $700,000 in assets. In his mind, this was more than enough, and it would have been, except after he retired, Norman ended up in a nursing home, and it was a very expensive place. In less than a year, he had spent every last bit of his money on his long term care, and nothing went to his daughter except for the house. He lost his entire life savings."

"That's really sad," Martha said.

"It is sad, but I don't want the same thing to happen to you. So, we should start thinking about this now while you're still healthy and able to get insured or find some other way of offsetting those potential costs."

> "According to recent statistics, 91% of Americans don't have long term care insurance! This is amazing to me, because odds are most of us will need care at some point in our lifetimes."

Luckily, Robert and Martha could see the wisdom in this right away, and it was easy getting them into a plan with better protections.

According to recent statistics in a Harris Poll survey, 91 percent of Americans don't have long term care insurance! This is amazing to me, because odds are most of us will need care at some point in our lifetimes. Mitigating this risk is especially critical for middle class and upper middle class Americans because the majority of them aren't below poverty level, and therefore do not qualify for insurance. I've known some that have paid hundreds of thousands of dollars out of pocket—upwards of $8,000 to $10,000 per month—in long term care costs, simply because they couldn't get insured, or just weren't prepared for the extra expenses.

Retirement planning isn't just envisioning your perfect wealth lifestyle of golfing on the weekends and spending more time with your grandkids, it's also planning for taxes, long term care costs, market losses, etc. Whether it's medical, tax planning, estate planning—all these things create a holistic picture of your retirement.

If your retirement planner isn't estimating how long you could feasibly pay for long term care before you've exhausted your life savings and they aren't actively trying to avoid that scenario—they aren't doing their job!

The Market

I have a client, her husband has $800,000 in his portfolio—it's all in the market, though.

He's all caught up in the paper amount—$800,000! It looks so good on paper. In reality, it's a paper illusion. Today his portfolio is worth $800,000, but tomorrow, who knows?

Everyone has a different tolerance for risk, but personally, I just don't think I could stomach that amount of pressure. Peace of mind is worth its weight in gold and being anxious about the markets can undermine your health and your marriage. I know men who won't even tell their wives how up or down they were in the market, because they were embarrassed. To me, that's a dangerous thing...

> "Making a profit as an investor is not fate, it's timing."

I warned her, if he keeps that money in the stock market, he could potentially lose $400,000 in the next downturn. Just like that. You look at your portfolio balance one day, and the next it's cut in half. While a younger person who is still in their working years can afford a high risk such as this, it makes a huge difference if you're retired and living off the interest of that account. It can really affect your lifestyle.

All throughout history there have been ups and downs in the market, and some cycles are more dramatic than others. Making a profit as an investor is not fate, it's timing. When you sell, when you buy—these things have a lot to do with how well you do. One person may run out of money and another person grows their money in leaps and bounds. It's all timing.

If you're relying on the market to provide income for your wealth lifestyle, it's a lot like rolling the dice. It may not work out. The question is, do you really want to bet your entire life savings, all you worked for over the last forty years on a crap shot? Obviously, it's not a very good idea when you're trying to make a sensible plan for retirement.

What if the markets crash and you have health issues, or your spouse becomes sick? It's a double whammy. You could have a financial living hell on your hands. What if it's a bad time to take your money out of the market, but you need to take it out to cover an emergency expense? Not a good idea.

The point is, you never really know what's coming around the corner, and that's why, when you plan for retirement, you need to take some of these big risks off the table, to avoid destroying everything you've worked so hard for. As long as your income base is set up properly, calculated risk is fine. But when it comes to the stock market, I always tell my clients, only risk what you can afford to lose.

There's a lot about life you can't control, like health, but you can control your finances.

Health

Speaking of health ... most people underestimate just how much health costs may increase in retirement. Even dental is a huge expense. What happens when you need implants, or you break a tooth? You have $10,000 in dental bills, suddenly. Health is a big expense in retirement that we usually don't plan for. There's a lot of wear and tear on the body as we age. What may seem like a minor thing now—such as a replacement crown—but can be very costly when you're older.

Things change. Our bodies change, the markets change, even our tax codes change. For instance, were you aware that Congress just passed the Secure Act in December 2019, and did away with inherited IRAs? Your kids cannot inherit your IRA now. And it happened just like that.

Purchasing Power

It is difficult to get an accurate read on the current inflation rates, because often certain things are taken out when they formulate those numbers. If you want to know how bad inflation has gotten, there's one surefire way to look at it—how much is it to buy a new car or pickup truck? If it's a full-sized Cadillac or BMW 3 Series, today, you could be paying somewhere between $60,000 and $100,000 per vehicle! Think of what those prices were even just ten years ago. According to friends of mine in the construction business, home building supplies are up 35 percent from five years ago. It's obvious that the prices have gone up, in a very tangible way, despite what the "official" numbers tell us.

My question is—is your money keeping up with that?

The importance of inflation becomes much more apparent to us in retirement, when we go to buy a new car, or make a repair on our home, or budget for our weekly groceries. The actual inflation rate may seem low, but we instinctively know our purchasing power has gone down. This is a huge, often overlooked, risk.

Using bank assets as an investment is unavoidable. We all need some bank assets, and a checking account to pay our bills, and we should have six months' savings, so we can feel comfortable. But in excess of that, if you have the bulk of your assets in the bank, or in a money market, you have a huge purchasing power risk. I like to call CDs "certificates of disappointment" because you may have the same $100,000 in your CD five to ten years later, but you can purchase a lot less with it than before.

To make things worse, our federal budget deficit is out of control. As of this writing, it stands at $26 trillion and growing. Not to mention, because of recent events (I'm writing this during the global pandemic), the U.S. government and Federal Reserve are pushing for even lower interest rates so we can remain competitive with the rest of the world. Once interest rates go to zero, we won't be able to earn anything on our money that is sitting in our bank accounts, and with the monetary policy going forward, it's only going to ensure that the prices of things are going up much faster than we've experienced before.

When we're talking about risk, purchasing power risk is a huge problem for retirees going forward. Many people, out of concern for the safety of their money, have gone to banks, credit unions, and put their money into money markets and savings accounts, but they don't understand the purchasing power risk that we have the answer for. With a better strategy for saving, we can have the ups of the markets, without the downs, and historically keep pace with inflation.

Mitigating risk is crucial.

What I'm saying is, people who have millions to spare can take all the risks they want, but if you're middle or even upper middle class, you can't afford to get taken off guard. As it is, it's hard enough to generate the income you'll need to enjoy a wealth lifestyle, and most Americans aren't starting their retirement planning from a position of preparedness.

According to the latest release from the Investment Company Institute, today, about 82 percent of all retirement plan assets are at risk due to the stock market. American workers don't have enough guaranteed pension income, and they're taking too many chances with their nest eggs. It's not entirely their fault, people are conditioned to do what they've always done, and they resist change. You may think you're all set for the next chapter in life, and in reality, you're not. I'm telling you it's fixable, but if you aren't open to making adjustments to your plan to accommodate the risks and realities of our day and age, you will likely be facing problems in your retirement.

Let's look at all the risks together and eliminate some of the dangers that can steal your peace of mind overnight, that's what I'm saying. Inflation, deflation, market losses, longevity risks, health care, withdrawal rate, tax risk, long term care, sequence of returns, market fluctuations—if you tackle all these things, you'll have an airtight plan to protect what you have.

There will come a day when no man or woman can work; nobody can work forever. If you've worked so hard to accumulate something of value, wouldn't it be devastating to lose it?

The most important thing is to protect what you've built up.

Now that we've covered risks—and hopefully I haven't scared you too much—let's do a deeper dive into one of the most important topics for retirement: leaving something behind, a legacy. Not just any legacy, a *tax advantaged* legacy.

CHAPTER 9

LEAVING A TAX ADVANTAGED LEGACY

One of my clients, a woman who lived on the coast of North Carolina, came to see me about a problem she was having with her estate planning. She had around $500,000 saved and wanted to pass that money on to her only daughter, but she wasn't sure the best way of going about it.

As her advisor, I encouraged her to consult with an attorney about setting up a trust so that when she passed, her daughter actually received $2,000,000, and it was completely tax free. No estate or inheritance taxes, no income or federal taxes. It was completely free money. Her daughter was so impressed, she said, "I want to work with you." Now we're working on her retirement and estate planning, so that her children can benefit from a tax advantaged legacy.

This is a big dilemma for retirees: How do you get your wealth to your children without Uncle Sam coming in and taking half?

It isn't magic, the trick is leveraging your money in a tax advantaged way, so you can pass it down to your heirs. How do you achieve that? Through life insurance, and other financial products. Life insurance for wealth transfer is the most common, and if you set up a life insurance plan properly, this is actually really easy to do.

Like I said, I don't create life insurance policies for all my clients (personally, I have a lot of life insurance, but that's me), but if it's a tool that can accomplish your goals and it works well for you—then let's do it. If life insurance isn't a good fit for you, there are plenty of other ways to achieve the same ends, such as government bonds, stocks, real estate, gifting, and trusts. For instance, if you're sitting on some stocks you've had forever, or matured government bonds, you can gift those to your children, or grandchildren. Looking at all the potential options for tax advantaged wealth transfer—it's really good planning.

Another big question my clients usually have is, when is the best time to protect your real estate assets?

I have some clients that do this later in life, with the intention of gifting their property to their heirs after they've passed. Others create a "life lease," where they don't own the property, but they have the right to stay in the home as long as they're alive. This works well for retirees, as it transfers the asset out of their name and taking the property out of your name means those assets are no longer on the table, they can't be liened or eaten up to pay for long term care costs or medical expenses.

> "Figure out what you'd like to pass down, whether that's real estate, a trust, or something else, and create a strategy for getting it to your heirs with the least amount of hassle or taxes being taken out."

The point is: you should look at all this ahead of time. Figure out what you'd like to pass down, whether that's real estate, a trust, or something else, and create a strategy for getting it to your heirs with the least amount of hassle or taxes being taken out. Like any type of plan, you'll have a much greater result if you start early.

Besides taxes, there are a few other things that could prevent your heirs from receiving the full sum of their inheritance. Here's some of them:

Leaving a Lump Sum

This is a big mistake—some clients leave it all in a lump sum to their kids. These are the folks who get hit the hardest with taxes. With strategic gifting and planning done ahead of time, you can mitigate that tax risk and get a much bigger sum of money to your heirs.

Longevity

We touched on this in the last chapter, but the biggest risk people have in retirement, other than the stock market, is the fact that today we are living much longer simply because of modern medicine and technology. There is a much greater need for long term care, especially for women, who statistically live longer than men. As I pointed out, long term care is crazy expensive, not to mention there's a general shortage of assisted living facilities—there aren't even enough places!

Most people who come to see me aren't covered for long term care by their insurance. They don't like to talk about it either—it's not a comfortable topic—so the tendency is to sweep it under the rug. Not taking into account your long term care costs could wipe out what you can pass down to your children, and it doesn't take long to blow through your entire savings.

Legal Documents

I'm not an attorney, but I'm definitely a motivator for people to get their legal documents in order. I cannot tell you how many meetings I've sat in on where I've had to refer a client to a good attorney because their legal documents are a mess—their will isn't up to date, in some cases the laws have changed in their state, or there's missing documents. Do their children know whether or not they'd like to be on life support, or should they pull the plug? Who is their power of attorney? Nobody knows because their documents don't reflect the current plan.

If they were to die tomorrow, their heir or heirs would have a big problem on their hands.

Having your legal documents current and up to date is crucial when talking about wealth transfer. Without realizing it, you could be putting your loved ones in a terrible position. What if your husband has a stroke, but he controls all the money in the estate? Chances are if you try to call the bank, they won't release any information because your name isn't on anything. You'd have to go to court just to get control of these assets. I've seen this happen to too many people.

No one is set up perfectly, and even I don't have all the answers, but I can tell you, I always find something amiss in people's legal docs, and most aren't set up correctly. So, get your documents in order!

Adjusting the Plan

I've had a lot of experience with wealth transfer. In fact, I work with many families, up to three generations of family members, that I have assisted in passing down their money to their heirs tax free. Currently, I'm handling a wealth transfer for a client, his sister, her sons, and their children. That's multiple generations of wealth transfer. And because I took the time to set up properly, there is no probate, their children are direct beneficiaries. That encompasses fifteen years of working with one single family.

One thing that I've learned over the course of my career, is that things change. And you have to adjust the plan, accordingly. What worked for one generation, may not be feasible for the next.

For instance, my client Ron Cooley.

Ron retired from DuPont with a nice pension and retirement savings. He never married and his sister was his only heir. When Ron passed, she inherited all the money in his IRAs. All that's changed now.

> "Just because something has changed doesn't mean I hang up my hat, or stop recommending clients use IRA's."

As I mentioned in the last chapter, in 2019 they passed the Secure Act, which has done away with stretch IRA's. In other words, what worked for Ron and his sister, is no longer available—no more stretch IRAs over beneficiaries' lifetime, now limited to 10 years. If you have $200,000 or more in retirement assets in an IRA, like Ron did, a change like this could really impact you.

Just because something has changed doesn't mean I hang up my hat or stop recommending clients use IRAs. I have to adjust the way I structure their wealth transfer plan, that's all. Throughout the years, we've had many changes to our tax and retirement laws. Most people don't know anything about this. It's my job to look at wealth transfer in light of tax code changes and inform clients of any recent changes to the laws, so they can make good decisions concerning their estate.

Some people's children are well off, and it won't make much of a difference whether they receive an inheritance or not. But if you aren't in this category of people, you should take these things into consideration now, so that you aren't putting your heirs in a bad position after you're gone. Ideally, you want a tax advantaged wealth transfer plan, one that is non-contestable, immediately available to your loved ones, with no income or estate taxes. One of the goals of a wealth lifestyle is peace of mind knowing your wealth is protected, not just for yourself, but for future generations.

CHAPTER 10

NOW IS THE TIME TO DREAM

There are two times in our lives when we dream: when we are young, and entering the world of adulthood for the first time, we wonder, *what am I going to do with my life?* Also, when we reach our 50-60s, again, we say, *I've lived my life, now what am I going to do with the rest of it?*

Retirement doesn't have to be a dreaded occurrence.

In our great grandparents' era, people used to die at age sixty-five, but now we live another twenty to twenty-five years. Are we supposed to just hang around waiting to die? That sounds dreadful. I don't know about you, but personally, there is only so much I can do sitting around. I would get bored since I do not play golf.

Retirement has changed, people don't want to "retire," they want to spend the next half of their lives being active and healthy and accomplishing their dreams. If you've gotten this far in your career, I'm willing to bet you have skills and talents you can still contribute to the world in a meaningful way. It's time to dream about what's next. What do you want to do?

Bill Gates is the quintessential example of what it looks like to dream. Gates basically said that his accomplishments in life 2.0 were going to be way more valuable and fulfilling than creating operating systems. Don't get me wrong, operating systems are good and all, but think about what the Gates's non-profit charitable foundation has been able to do on a global scale.

Let me give you another example. My friend Chris is a bright guy, Harvard MBA, and a very diligent and committed Christian. When he made enough money that he didn't have to work anymore, he could have just said, "I'm retiring." Instead, he waited four years and then volunteered as the CEO of a nonprofit ministry called Opportunity International. He found his niche. Under his watch, he grew the organization, securing microloans for people in poverty all over the world. In 2009, Chris invited me to help him fund independent schools in sub-Saharan Africa and provide them small business loans, training, and consulting. Fast forward ten years, and Opportunity International is in eleven different countries, 3,500 schools, with over a million students.

In the last ten years, it's the most rewarding and inspirational thing we've ever done. I wasn't going to go quietly into retirement. I wanted to take our God given gifts and make a difference in the world.

Even at a young age, I always knew that I wanted to dedicate a portion of my life to giving back. Because you always get back more than you give.

When I was in my thirties, a couple of years after my car wreck, I took a two-week vacation. My work was so intense at that time, I only had two weeks off for the whole year. What did I decide to do with my time? Lay on a beach working on my tan? Nope. I counseled at a summer camp.

The camp was for young boys, aged ten to teens. There were so many great things that happened that week. Even though I was isolated from my family, and from my work, I cannot believe how much it blessed me and helped me, even though I was helping others. I saw these boys' lives change before my eyes. After that camp experience, from that point on, I was always involved in something, singing in a church choir, ministering, doing charity motorcycle runs, or supporting my business partner, Hal, while he went on Christian missions all over the world. One time, he even managed to get me to go on a mission with him. We went to the Caribbean and I stayed behind after the church service to minister to people who were waiting in line for two or three hours just to have someone pray with them. These memories stand out in my mind, they are some of the most incredible experiences in my life.

Finding your purpose is a lot like finding your soulmate. For some, passing a legacy on to their grandchildren is enough. For others, they may want a larger challenge. Very few people would tell you their career is their real purpose in life. Most people would like to somehow make a difference.

I'm an avid motorcyclist. A few years ago, I did a charity motorcycle ride from Michigan to Georgia. The event wasn't cheap, it was $15,000 per person, but the most amazing thing about the ride was that it was filled with type A personalities. There were celebrities, successful athletes, entrepreneurs, race car drivers and motorheads from all over the world. These were go-getters. None of these people were done with their lives. None of them were the typical "retiree." Sure, they want to play golf and hang out with their grandkids, but they also want to do something bigger.

Successful people have similar qualities. For people like us who have been go-getters all our lives, they don't know how to stop. If they stop, they die.

The point is, when we surrender to God's plan, instead of our own, there's so much richness and fulfillment in life. Retirement isn't just about buying a new Porsche. A Porsche is great and all, but you might get that new car and think life is going to be grand, and then you'll wreck the car and end up in the hospital and God's plan takes over.

It's time to do what you feel you're being called to do. What does this next chapter look like? What does fulfillment look like? If you could only do one thing every day, what would it be? How important is golf? How important are cruises? How important are new cars? Material wealth is only 8 percent of your life. What do you want that other 92 percent of your life to be about? If the answer is family, then do it right, do it wonderfully. But if you want to change the world, now is the time to do it.

What is the story you're going to create—the unique thing that God wants you to do with the rest of your life?

Just as a young man or woman, when you let your thoughts and visions take you far into an imagined future, now is the time to carve a new path. Think bigger. You don't have to check in with the HR department or get permission from your boss or put in a request for vacation time. What are those experiences that you'd like to have? That's the gift of retirement. If you've planned well financially and followed the advice in this book, you now have an opportunity to do whatever you like. What are you going to do with it?

Now is the time!

CHAPTER 11

LET'S GET STARTED

Maybe you think you're already all set, or maybe you think you're too far behind, or maybe you haven't put much thought into your retirement planning at all. None of that should stop you from taking one step toward creating the wealth lifestyle you want.

What does one step forward look like? It looks like an email (or a phone call if you're old school). It looks like me getting a little information about you and where you're at right now, and finding out where you'd like to go, and then creating a road map for you to get there.

Why do I put so much importance on getting to know you?

If I were to give you an address in Charlotte, North Carolina, how do you get there if you don't know where you're starting from? Are you in Boston? Florida? If you don't know where you currently are, you might take a wrong turn and head south instead of north. You'll never reach your destination. So, figuring out what your current situation looks like is essential to creating a blueprint, and it's something you can start right now, and it won't cost you a penny.

But you have to take that first step.

It may seem like a lot of things are stopping you, but usually those turn out to be excuses. Here are some of the most common arguments I've heard:

I'm Already Taken Care Of

Many people think because they already have an advisor, they don't need to go through the Wealth Lifestyle Method. Well, all I have to say to that is, just like some people have multiple doctors—general doctors, heart doctors, ER doctors—there are also different types of advisors in the financial world. Do you have a stock market advisor? Or a wealth lifestyle advisor? If all you have is one advisor, how can you get a second opinion? Or maybe you have a great advisor but he's not an expert in taxes, growth, safety, or estate planning. You may want to add a "specialist" to your team.

I Have Lots of Money, I Should Be Fine

This is another phrase I hear a lot.

Sure, you may have a lot of money now, and you're successful, but does your current plan have protection from market crashes, taxes, inflation, health care, long term care, expenses, and longevity risks? And does your current plan maximize your guaranteed income from the money you've saved? Maybe you're currently getting 2.8 percent from your nest egg, would you like to double or triple that number?

I'm Too Far Behind

This is really sad when I hear this, but all too common.

Some people feel like they've waited too long and there's no hope, and they're amazed when they sit down with me and find out there are still a lot of things that can be done to amplify and multiply the wealth they do have.

Those strategies are unique to each person, but there are effective tactics for older adults to increase their wealth without relying on the stock market alone, and many creative strategies to help their money to go further and give them more peace of mind. If you feel you're too far behind, then it's imperative you contact us as soon as possible so we can get started on this today, before it really is too late!

What Will It Cost Me?

Nothing, the initial consultation is free of charge, and if you want to put together a plan with us, great, but if not, then that's fine, too. I want clients, sure, but I also want the right type of clients. It has to be a good fit for both of us.

I Don't Know Where To Begin!

It's easy to fall into this state of being totally overwhelmed when thinking about retirement. The general public is totally out of their league. That's exactly why you need an advisor. We do all of that heavy lifting for you. You don't have to become a financial wizard, or manage your own money, or read ten thousand books, or become a stock market pro. We use what I call "autopilot strategies," once implemented, you do not need to babysit them.

And finally, the biggest reason why things don't get done? People procrastinate; that's human nature.

That has to stop now. You've worked hard your whole life, slaved away ten, twenty, thirty years for your retirement. That's decades of sitting in the morning commute, missing out on events, taking less days off, scrimping and saving, and passing up on some of the things you'd really like to be doing instead of saving up this money. Isn't it worth twenty minutes of your time to protect all that hard work?

Retirement is like building a beautiful sand castle on the beach. It's gorgeous, until the tide comes and takes it out. Not only should you have a clear path forward to your ideal wealth lifestyle, once you've gone through the initial process of making goals, tallied up your expenses and figured out an income base, and mitigated risk—now that you've done all that, don't you want someone who can show you how to actually protect it?

I'm guessing you wouldn't have made it this far in the book if you weren't at least a little bit inclined to begin building your wealth lifestyle. So, I've included a link for my website, where you can find our Wealth Lifestyle Fact Finder: https://stevenmengland.com/. Just a simple online questionnaire that you can fill out, with no obligations. Even if you decide you don't want to go any further with this method, taking this one step is a great way to learn a little bit more about yourself and your retirement goals.

So, let's get started, shall we?

Made in United States
North Haven, CT
10 November 2026

22088889R00076